300
WRITING
PROMPTS

Sarah Evans

Every secret of a writer's soul, every experience of his life, every quality of his mind is written large in his works.
- Virginia Woolf

"Your Favorites"

"About You"

"You Have the Control"

"Friendships and Relationships"

"Think About It"

"Reflect / The Past"

"Your Favorites"

What is your favorite smell? What does it make you think of?

What is your favorite emotion to display? Why?

Write an alternate ending to your favorite book or movie.

What is your favorite fictional world and would you want to live there? Why or why not?

Who is your favorite author? What are some questions you would ask them if you could meet them?

Do you find more value in winning an argument or being likable? Why?

What is your favorite color and what significance do you think it bears on your life?

What is your favorite room in your house? Why?

What is your favorite hobby and why should more people enjoy your hobby?

Who is your favorite historical figure and why?

What is your favorite musical instrument to listen to? Why?

Who is your favorite actor/actress? Name a movie or TV show they were in that you did not like. Why didn't you like it?

What is your favorite book that hasn't been adapted for film yet? Do you want to see it become a movie? Why or why not?

Describe your ideal road trip. Where would you go? Who would you take with you? How long would you be gone?

What is the perfect way to spend your birthday?

Describe your perfect vacation.

What does your ideal Saturday night look like?

What season do you look forward to and why?

What would you put on the ultimate sandwich?

What is your favorite instrument and why?

Do more toppings make a pizza better or is it best to have fewer? What is your reasoning?

Which food group would you hate to give up? Why?

What is the funniest joke you have heard lately?

What combination of flavors would make the ultimate flavor of ice cream?

Describe your perfect day at work.

Who is your favorite fictional character? What qualities do you love about them?

Who is your favorite person, living/dead, famous/not and why?

What is your favorite condiment? What is something unconventional you eat it on?

Describe your favorite dessert.

Who is your favorite fictional character and what stance would they take on climate change?

Describe your favorite flower, plant, or tree. Why is it your favorite?

What is your favorite band? Describe the first time you heard their music.

Describe your ideal role at your perfect job.

What is your favorite thing about summer?

Name some little things that can make your day great.

How do you take your coffee?

What is your favorite flavor to add to hot chocolate?

If money were no object, describe what your dream home would look like.

What car would you like to drive, but, not own? Why wouldn't you want to own it?

If you could learn any musical instrument proficiently overnight, what would it be and why?

What dance or dance style would you like to learn? Why?

Describe the best concert/show you have ever been to.

What is your addiction? What would make you overcome it?

What color do you think should be removed from the color wheel (and thus never used)? Why?

Describe your favorite meal. Would you eat this meal every day? Why or why not?

Describe your perfect first date, start to finish.

What is your favorite movie and why do you like it?

Describe the perfect day at the beach.

What was the best gift you ever gave?

What is the most interesting story you have heard?

"About You"

What is one thing about you that you would never change?

Name 5 things that can make your day great.

Is having power over someone more important than having his or her respect?

What would be on a flag that represents you?

Are you a night owl or an early bird? What are some benefits to being the opposite?

If you were on a pirate ship, what would your job be?

Pretend you are competing in a talent competition. Describe your act/routine.

What about your look/appearance is distinctly you?

What helps you think? (i.e. pacing, tapping, music)

What do you do when you know you have failed at something?

What do you do when you see an insect or spider indoors?

Do you prefer physical books or digital ones? Why?

What role do you typically take in a group project? Why do you think that is?

Which aspect do you value more – beauty or brains? Why?

What motivates you to exercise?

Do you wish you were born somewhere else? Where and why?

Would you rather sky dive or scuba dive? Why?

Is it more important to be honest with yourself or with those around you? Why?

What is a class you wish you could have taken in school? Why?

What are 5 of your favorite foods? What do you think these 5 foods say about you?

What is something you wish people could understand about you?

What is the most pointless fact you know? How did you come to know this fact?

What TV show would you want to live in? Why?

Would you rather work for a cruise line or an airline? Why?

Do you prefer that poems rhyme? Why or why not?

In a fantasy world, are you more likely to be a knight, an archer, or a mage? Why?

When you are both hungry and tired, which do you typically give into first? Why?

Describe qualities of a new food that might prevent you from trying it. Is it the look? Smell? Texture?

What aspects of your personality are you most proud of? Why?

Describe what you imagine when you "go to your happy place".

What is your favorite day of the week and what makes it so special?

How do you react when someone tells you that you are incapable of doing something?

What is the legacy you wish to leave behind? How do you intend to accomplish this?

How would you describe your pace when walking? Is there a pace people take you find frustrating?

What emotion are you most embarrassed to display? Why?

What do you think it means to "wear your heart on your sleeve"? Are you guilty of doing this? Why or why not?

Do you think more women should wear make-up? Why or why not?

How do you describe your body type? Are you happy with your body type? Why or why not?

What movie best describes your life? In what ways is this true?

What fictional character do you resonate with the most? Why?

What is one thing you wish you could change about your routine? Why?

Is there something at your job you are bad at? How can you improve?

Which season do you think impacts your mood the most? Why?

How might you improve your greatest flaw?

What song accurately describes how you feel about yourself? Why?

What "sense" do you think you could live without?

Which of the following do you think you could get rid of: radio, TV, or internet? How might it impact your day-to-day?

What is your most commonly-used nickname and how do you feel about it?

What is the most interesting thing about you?

Do you believe in ghosts? Why or why not?

What fabric do you prefer to wear the most? Why?

"You Have the Control"

Create your own quote and explain it.

If you could communicate with any animal, which would it be and why?

Would you rather be able to fly or teleport – why?

Would you rather live in a place that is extremely hot or extremely cold? Describe what you would do on your typical day in your chosen climate.

Should there be more or fewer holidays? What holiday(s) would you add or take away?

What would you do if you were in charge of the world for a day?

Would you prefer that your favorite musician stops making music or that your favorite show gets canceled? Why?

Make up a word, its meaning, its part of speech, and its origin.

NASA has given you the task of renaming the planets in our solar system. What do you name them?

You have been crowned the leader of the world. What is your first act as leader?

Would you name your kids after celebrities? How about fictional characters? If yes to either, what would you name them?

Do you want to visit another planet? Which one and why?

What special skill do you wish you had? What would you do with it?

If you could eliminate one season, what would it be and why?

If you could create a new month, what would you call it and where would you put it? How many days would it have?

Would you rather have the ability to go backwards or forwards in time? Why?

You've been nominated to represent Earth during a visit with aliens from outer space. What might you tell the aliens to communicate that Earthlings are peaceful?

Name a living creature you hate (i.e. spider, snake, etc.). Given the choice, would you have it completely eradicated from Earth? Why or why not?

Would you rather have steak or ice cream right now? Why?

If you knew the world was going to end tomorrow, what would be your last meal?

How would you go about ending world hunger?

How would you spend a billion dollars?

If you were a lawyer, would you focus on being moral or on winning every case? Why?

What is one thing you would change about the internet if you could?

How would you arrange the alphabet if you could change it? Why?

If you could rewrite, add, or remove any law, what would it be and why?

8 hours is the recommended amount of sleep that the human body needs to function. If you could change this, what would you change the number to and why?

Would you want to have an identical twin? Why or why not? (If you are a twin, would you want to not be a twin?)

You've been chosen to make the lead float for a parade! Describe what your float would look like and how it would function.

If you could swap any body part for a mechanical equivalent (i.e. swapping an arm for a rocket launcher), what would it be and why?

Many restaurants offer a "soup de jour" or soup of the day. You always hope it is something you like, but oftentimes that falls flat. Name a soup that you would want banned from "soup de jour" and explain why you chose that soup.

If you had to choose, would you rather eliminate surfaces you can sit on (chairs, couches) or surfaces you set stuff on (tables, counters)? Explain your answer.

Would you accept an offer of always having good luck if it meant someone in the world would always have bad luck? What if it was guaranteed to be someone in your family? Explain your answers.

How long do you think vacations should be? Why?

If given the choice, would you like to be driven around for the rest of your life, but sacrifice your ability to drive? Why or why not?

If given the control, would you have all forms of hunting banned? Why or why not?

What 3 phrases would you teach a talking parrot?

Would you rather travel (for vacation) somewhere snowy, beachy, or in the middle of nowhere? Why?

Do you consider modern day humans to be predators? Why or why not?

Would you rather be a northerner or southerner? Why?

What is one thing you could be a "guru" of? How would you impart your knowledge on others?

If you could permanently change the pitch of your voice, would you make it higher or lower? Why?

What would you do if you were president for a day?

Would you ban guns if you could? Why or why not?

If you were leader of the world, would you ban war? Why or why not?

What would you do if you woke up the opposite gender you are now?

If you could stop aging at a specific age, which age would it be and why?

If you could have any band (still together or otherwise) play at your house for a private concert, who would you pick and why?

If you could cause any one type of natural disaster to be eradicated (i.e. floods, tornados, etc.) which would you get rid of and why?

If you could get rid of one insect without unbalancing the ecosystem, which would you get rid of and why?

"Friendships and Relationships"

Write a letter to a friend you have not seen in a long time.

Can a person have more than one best friend? Why or why not?

Is having power over someone more important than having their respect? Why?

What 3 words would you use to describe your driving? What 3 words would your best friend use to describe your driving?

Can a person have more than one true love? Why or why not?

What are the 5 most important qualities of a friendship?

What are 25 small ways you can demonstrate that you care about someone without spending a dime?

Write about the last fight you had with a friend. How did it resolve? If it hasn't resolved, how do you expect it will resolve?

Which is more important – honesty or loyalty? Why?

What are some things that someone would be surprised to learn about you?

Think of the 5 people closest to you. Describe each using one word.

Which is worse – being too affectionate or not being affectionate enough? Why?

What fictional couple is your #goals relationship? Why?

Which fiction friends are your #goals friendship? Why?

How much of who you are is a product of who others expect you to be?

Would you call out of work, simply because your best friend asked you to, or wouldn't you? Why?

Who is so close to you that you could call them your shadow? How do you feel about your friendship/relationship?

Tell the story about a friend you became friends with in a weird or funny way.

Which of your friends is the most critical? What is one thing you wish you could say to them?

Is there anyone in your family you would be friends with if you weren't related? Who is it and what about your relationship makes you feel that way?

What will the relationship between you and your best friend look like in 10 years? 20 years?

Do you believe in soulmates? Why or why not?

Which celebrity would you be most interested in going on a date with? Describe the date.

Which friend do you feel most confident about being roommates with? What do you expect would be the most difficult aspect in living with them?

Do you feel that a friendship ending can feel worse than a romantic relationship ending? Why or why not?

Tell the story of the first time you met your best friend.

Describe a time that you helped a friend when you probably shouldn't have.

Describe each person in your group of friends using only one word.

Think of a time when you had to confront a friend or significant other when you were mad. How did you confront them? Explain how the confrontation resolved.

Which friend would you feel confident about if you got lost in the wilderness together? Why? Which friend do you feel like you met only coincidentally? What is one thing that could have happened differently to prevent you from meeting them?

Write a short story about you and your best friend waking up after a sleep over, having mysteriously switched bodies.

How would you and your best friend spend time together trapped indoors due to a blizzard (without internet!)?

Describe a time when you were far from your significant other.

Tell a story about a time your significant other gave you a gift you weren't too happy about.

Write about the first fight you had with your significant other.

How might your significant other respond to reading your diary or journal?

Do you think your significant other should also be your best friend? Why or why not?

Describe a time when your significant other didn't keep a promise. How did it make you feel?

Was your first kiss magical? Why or why not?

Describe a time when your best friend was being rotten to you. How did your friendship recover?

Write about a belief you and your significant other or best friend do not share. How do you navigate your relationship around this difference in opinion?

Would you describe your relationship with your best friend as "easy"? Why or why not?

Would you rather your significant other be funny and kind or intelligent and spontaneous? Why?

Was there a time when you thought your significant other was uninterested? How did you handle that?

Write about an inside joke you and your best friend have.

In what ways could your friend be compared to the word "glass"?

Write about a time when you didn't believe your best friend when he/she told you something. How did it turn out?

What is your favorite activity to do with your friends?

Would you rather your best friend be honest or loyal? Why?

"Think About It"

Write about a day in the life of a pencil.

Write a short story about a banana.

If you could, would you want to have a pet dinosaur? What kind? How would you take care of it?

Imagine that you lived with your least favorite fictional character. Write a scene depicting breakfast at your house.

What are some things you'd still be able to do really well if you only had 1 finger?

Write 5 compliments about someone you don't like.

Compare your worst physical pain with your worse emotional pain. Which would you say was worse?

Would you want a raccoon as a pet? Why or why not?

Sum up the world in one sentence.

What do you think a fish would say if it could talk?

Write a short story from the perspective of a villain, anti-hero, or an-
tagonist.

Is it possible for something to be "perfect"? Why?

In what circumstances might you risk your life for a complete stranger?

If you were an assassin, what would your weapon of choice be? Why do you think it would be the most effective for assassination?

What age, if ever, should most people stop watching cartoons?

Select a random object near you. Write a commercial for it.

List 3 or more things that have gone well today.

What is the first thing you think of when you see the number "101"?

Write a question you will never know the answer to. Why do you think you'll never know the answer?

Make up an "origin story" for a stranger you met recently.

Which type of weather tells the best stories? Why?

Can too much of a bad thing be good? Why or why not?

What do you think life will be like 500 years from now?

Write a short poem or story about the word "torn."

Is it worse to hold in your anger or let your anger explode? Why?

Do you wish healthcare was free? Why or why not?

Write the plot outline for your favorite Disney movie if you had been the main character. Consider what major decisions you would have made differently and how they might have impacted the ending.

If you were a teacher, what subject would you teach and how would you teach it?

How do you feel about "ginormous" being added to the dictionary?

Write a diary entry as though you were a monkey in zoo.

How would you handle someone threatening you and being aggressive towards you, but not coming into physical contact with you?

Write a story about a fictional town where everything is the opposite.

Do you think sugar is as harmful as drugs? Why or why not?

Write a short story depicting how tension can be toxic between two family members.

How might a toad handle crossing the street?

Describe a time you witnessed something unusual happening to someone else.

How do you think a camera has changed the way life is today compared to 250 years ago?

Would you still eat chicken if the talked like parrots? Why or why not?

Write a short story about an aquatic adventure featuring a captain who has never been on a boat before.

Define the word "dapper" and explain how it should be used.

Write a scene where a monkey tries to rob a bank.

How might a documentary be considered entertaining?

Do you think it is more important to be friendly or funny? Why?

Do you think it is more important to be skillful or open-minded when approaching most tasks? Why?

What is the most colorful meal you can remember having? What made it so colorful?

Write a story about a village (and its inhabitants) that reside within a bubble.

Explain the importance of grieving.

Why is it important to have a "system" in place before you start writing an essay, thesis, or novel?

Is it bad to be materialistic? Why or why not?

How do you think snow positively impacts an environment?

"Reflect / The Past"

Describe a time that you cried tears of joy.

What do you miss about your childhood?

Write about a compulsive purchase you made recently. Why do you think you bought that item compulsively?

What has changed the most about you since you were a child?

Describe something you foolishly believed as a child.

Who is someone you would like to reconnect with from your child-hood? Why?

What was something you wanted growing up that you never got? Why do you think your parents wouldn't give it to you?

Write about a time in your childhood when you were the most comfortable in your own skin, as your own person.

Describe a time you were really excited for something that didn't end up happening. How did you react and respond?

Think of a time when you refused something or refused to do something. Why did you refuse and how did the other person react?

What was it like your first time flying in a plane?

When you were growing up, who would you look to the most for wisdom? Why?

Describe what it was like learning to whistle.

Write about a time you felt anxious.

What is the oddest memory you keep from your childhood?

What is something you wish you had done when you were younger, and possibly more capable?

Have you ever punched someone? What prompted you to punch them?

Do you think you were more likeable as a child or do you think you are more likeable now? Why?

Describe a time when you received a gift you were completely surprised (and happy) about receiving.

Describe a time when you felt tough.

What chores did you have growing up? How did you feel about your chores?

Would you describe yourself as "unbiased"? Why or why not?

Write about a time when you doubted yourself, but persevered, and the outcome was good.

Describe a time when you felt weak. How did you recover?

Do you feel like you get enough sleep? What would you attribute as the cause to your answer?

Would you describe yourself as "cynical"? Why or why not?

What was something you looked forward to as a child, in terms of becoming an adult?

Have you ever cried from happiness? If so, what prompted it?

Who do you feel was the biggest influence during your upbringing? Why?

What is something you refused to eat as a child?

Do you feel like your parents were too controlling? Why or why not?

Describe a recent time where someone you know was impolite. How did you handle the situation?

Write about a time you felt victorious.

Describe your first time trying to drive a car.

Write a story, embellishing a time you were frantic about something.

What is an experience from your childhood you love to talk about?

What was it like learning to ride a bike for the first time?

Describe a time something creepy happened to you.

What is something about being older that is disappointing to your inner child?

Write about the last time you performed or gave a speech in front of more than 10 people.

What subject did you love during middle school? Why?

Is there a food you hated as a child, but love now? What do you think changed?

Describe a time you felt incredibly supported by someone you love.

Write about your most memorable teacher. What made them so memorable?

What do you value the most about family and friendships?

How do you personally measure value in a person?

Describe a time you did something you consider "neighborly".

Write a story about a verbal fight you had with someone, except, instead of you fighting with the person, you are fighting with a dragon.

Would you rather laugh or cry tears of joy? Why?

Write about something you used to collect as a child.

Made in the USA
Middletown, DE
16 December 2017